YOUR TASK

You have bailed out of your damaged spaceship over the Planet of Terror, and now you must find where it crashed. Each time you choose a new path, you will be told which page to turn to next. But there are many dangers on the planet. Sometimes you can overcome them by finding your way through a maze or by finding something hidden in the picture. Often you have to use your wits. All you have with you is a ray gun, which you can use on only one occasion. Your sole companion is ME2, a mechanical monkey who is not always very helpful! Whatever happens, you cannot turn back. Good luck!

First published 1985 by Walker Books Ltd
87 Vauxhall Walk, London SE11 5HJ

This edition published 2003

2 4 6 8 10 9 7 5 3 1

Text © 1985 Patrick Burston
Illustrations © 1985 Alastair Graham

The right of Patrick Burston and Alastair Graham to be identified as author and illustrator respectively of this work has been asserted by them in accordance with the Copyright, Designs and Patents Act 1988

This book has been typeset in Galliard

Printed in Hong Kong

All rights reserved

British Library Cataloguing in Publication Data:
a catalogue record for this book is
available from the British Library

ISBN 0-7445-9468-5

THE PLANET OF
TERROR

PATRICK BURSTON

illustrated by

ALASTAIR GRAHAM

WALKER BOOKS
AND SUBSIDIARIES
LONDON • BOSTON • SYDNEY

In a moment you and ME2 will land on a plateau in the wilderness of Terror. Choose a path that takes you on to page 7 to see which way to go.

If you arrive here turn to page 10.

If you arrive here turn to page 8.

A bottomless canyon yawns at your feet! Find the path that leads to the only point where you can cross. (Trace along the path with your finger.)

If you choose to go up this way turn to page 14.

If you decide to go down this way turn to page 12.

Deadly Tentaclons block your path!
If you touch them you will die. Can
you find a safe path between the tentacles?
(Trace a path with your finger.)

Turn to
page 16.

Turn to
page 14.

To get by those fierce,
stinging Heliflies you need
the help of their enemies,
the Hopsnappers. Only one
Hopsnapper is attacking the
Heliflies. Find the other
four and wake them up.

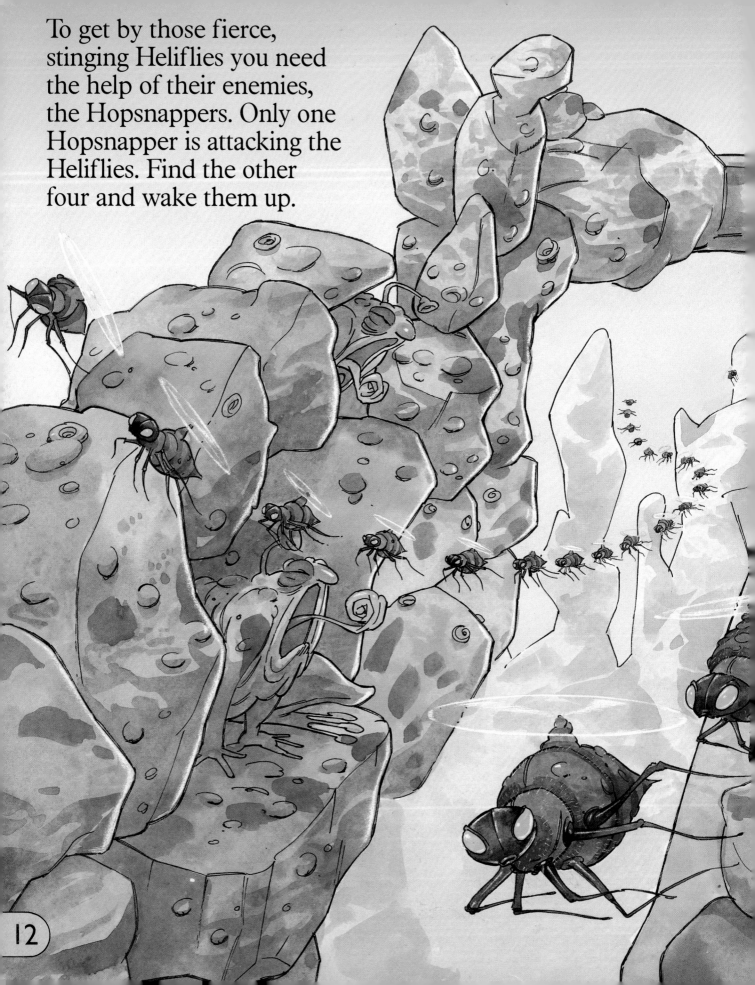

Now which way?
If you go down the rocky
staircase turn to page 20.
If you decide to go along
the rocky bridge turn
to page 18.

You feel exhausted.
You must eat.
The only fruit that is
safe to eat is a green
one that the alien animals
are *not* eating. Find it
and you will have the
strength to go on.

If you take the path
behind the fruit trees
turn to page 22.
If you go straight on
turn to page 20.

You have entered Terror City.
Ten hidden cameras watch you.
Locate and eliminate each one with
a burst from your ray gun. Then find
a way through the maze of tunnels.
(Trace a path with your finger.)

Turn to
page 24.

Turn to
page 22.

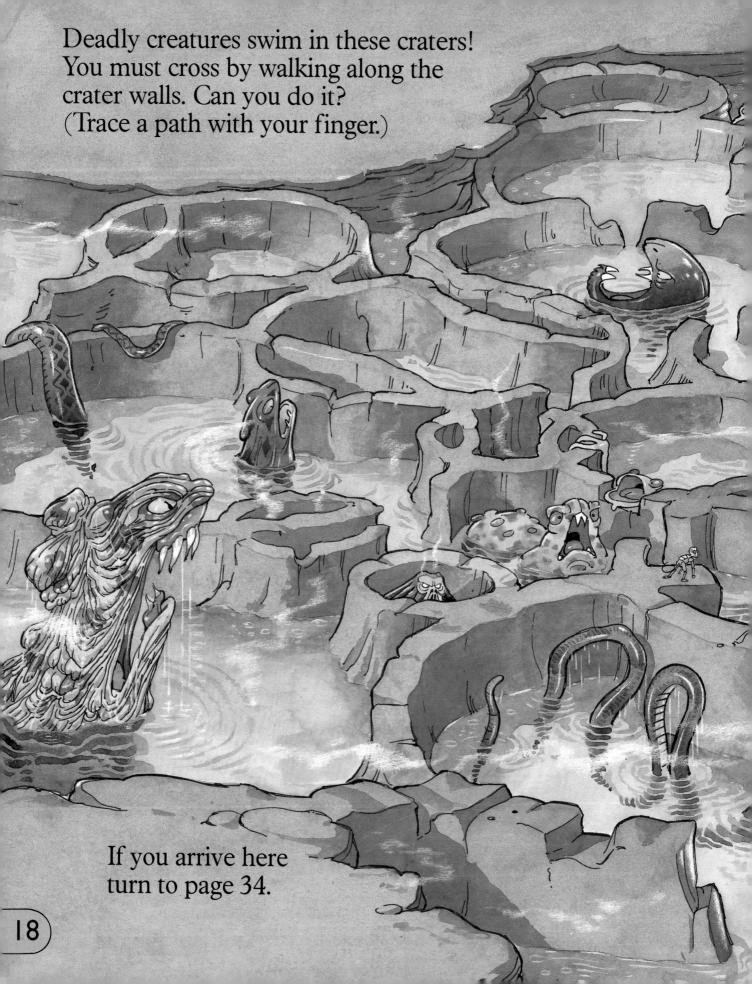

Deadly creatures swim in these craters!
You must cross by walking along the
crater walls. Can you do it?
(Trace a path with your finger.)

If you arrive here
turn to page 34.

18

If you arrive here
turn to page 26.

Inside Terror City a matter-transporter beam turns you into a stream of electrons. Start at the arrow and follow the circuit until you re-materialise!

Turn to
page 30.

Turn to
page 28.

You must sneak past these five ghastly Mutoids. Each Mutoid is a cross between two Earth animals. Do you recognise all ten original animals?

The door
leads to
page 32.

Take the
path to
page 30.

23

Somewhere in this scrapyard of space junk there are two Flotabikes. Find one and fly it to the page number painted on its side.

The Alpha robots are attacking the Zetas! Escape to the page given by adding up the numbers painted on either the Alpha or Zeta robots.

You have entered a low-gravity zone and haven't got enough energy to get down. So grab the heaviest boot you can find to help you get your feet back on Terror. (Pull in ME2 too!)

If you choose this path turn to page 36.

If you choose
this path turn
to page 38.

A Jelloid Blob lies in your path.
Its festering fingers are crushing
the space station. Find a pedestrian
walkway that is still passable,
but hurry!

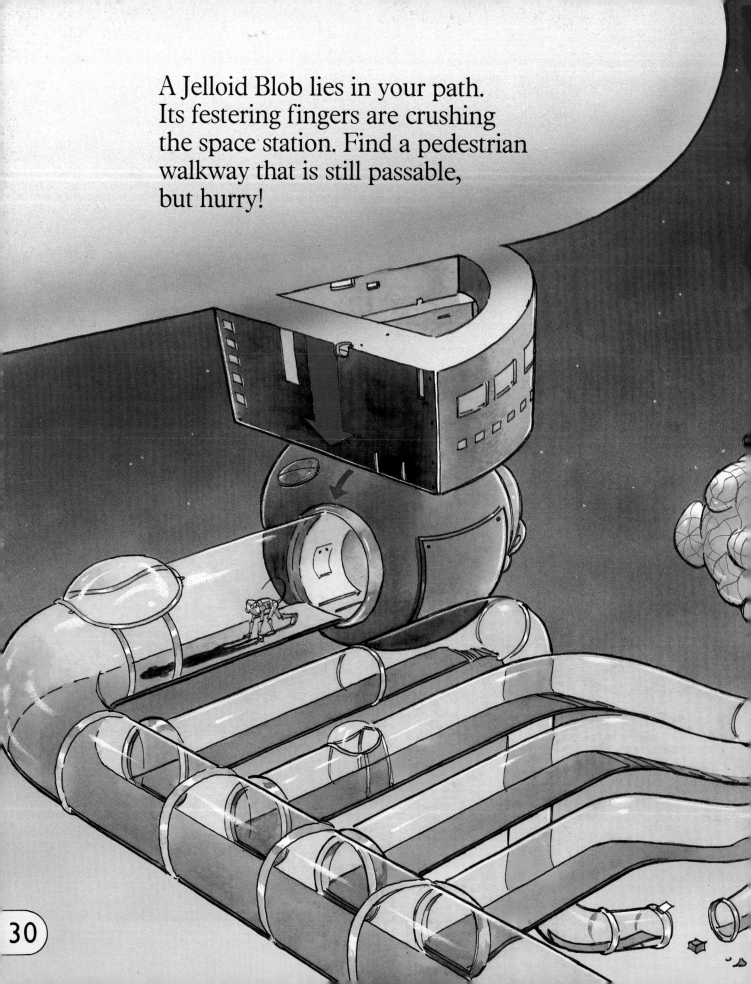

Turn to
page 40.

Turn to
page 38.

The evil Brain
of Terror has
its eye on you.
To pass by it
you must switch
off its life-support
cable. Which
one is it?

This door leads outside to page 42.

This door leads to a room on page 40.

The aliens want to trick you into thinking this is Earth, but they've made ten mistakes. See if you can find them.

If you go up the street, turn to page 42.
If you go right, turn to page 44.

The edge of the planet. Dead end! And you have lost ME2! Somewhere in the sky are four communication satellites in a square formation. If you spot them you will be able to send a signal to ME2. But to find your spaceship you must go back to page 6 and start again.

You have accidentally triggered a Doomsday Bomb that will destroy the planet! Quickly find the key to turn off the time clock. To find your spaceship, however, you must go back to page 6 and start again.

Too bad! You must go back to page 6 and start again.
But how do you get the doors to open? Only by spotting three differences between them! (Look round the edges.)

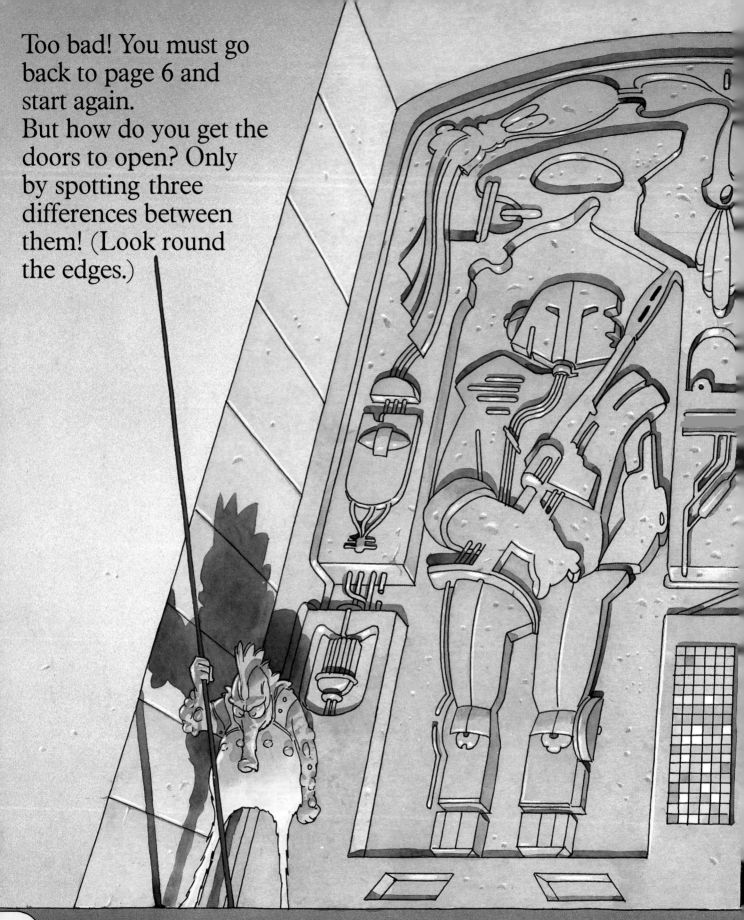

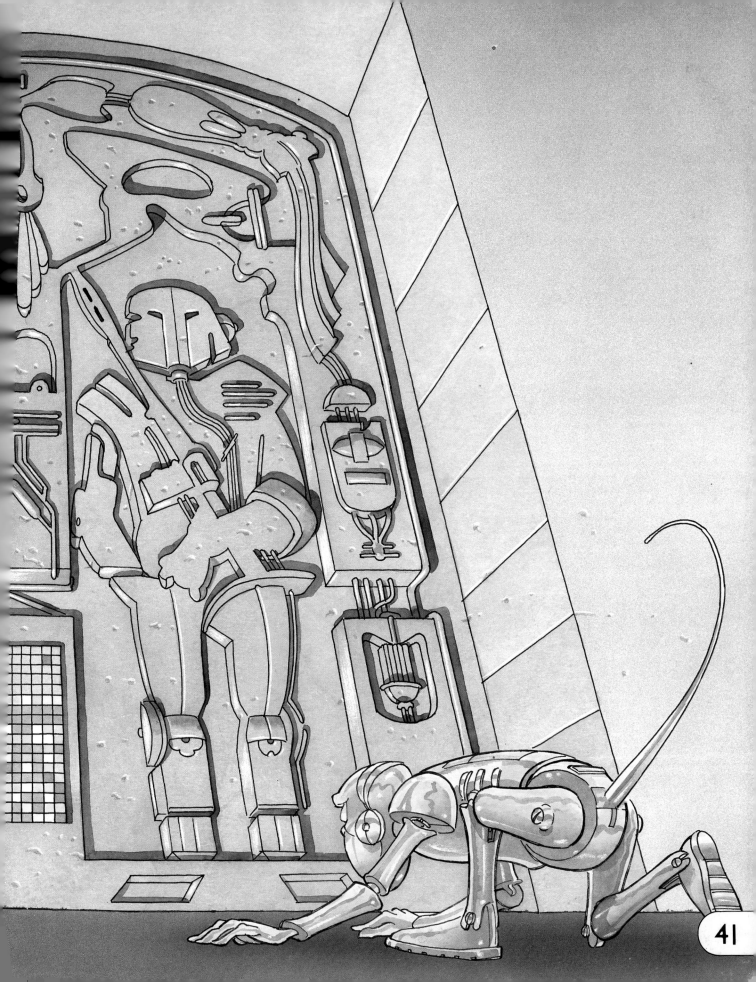

You have reached the
impassable Monster Mountains!
You must go back to page 6 and start
again. Find the mountain that looks like
a lion's head from a certain angle and
go down the cave formed by
the animal's mouth.

At last! There is your spaceship, the *Homestar*. But to repair it you have to find three missing pieces of the tail fin.

NOW
BLAST OFF
FOR EARTH!

Answers

22-23
tiger/eagle
rhinoceros/crocodile
buffalo/frog
snake/grasshopper
deer/snail

26-27
Alpha robots 36
Zeta robots 38

32-33
yellow cable

34-35
- no hands on clock
- three arms on statue
- no roots on tree
- square wheels on car
- no name on street sign
- lamp is a goldfish bowl
- steps lead to a window
- window has a door knocker
- light bulbs planted in window-box
- zebra crossing should be black-and-white and further from the corner
- drain grid should be at right-angles to pavement
- no kerb stones